STICK OUT YOUR TONGUE!

Make Me Laugh!

STICK OUT YOUR TONGUE!

jokes about doctors and patients

For Dawn – I hope these jokes tickle your funny bones!

Peter Roop

by Peter & Connie Roop / pictures by Joan Hanson

Lerner Publications Company · Minneapolis

For Susie, our favorite doctor,
who is "patient" with our punning

This book is available in two editions:
Library binding by Lerner Publications Company
Soft cover by First Avenue Editions
241 First Avenue North
Minneapolis, Minnesota 55401

Library of Congress Cataloging-in-Publication Data

Roop, Peter.
  Stick out your tongue!

  (Make me laugh!)
  Summary: A collection of jokes about doctors and
patients, such as "Why did the man laugh during his
operation? The doctor had him in stitches."
  1. Medicine-Juvenile humor. 2. Wit and humor,
Juvenile. [1. Medicine—Wit and humor. 2. Jokes.]
I. Roop, Connie. II. Hanson, Joan, ill. III. Title.
IV. Series.
PN6231.M4R66   1986   818´.5402   86-2940
ISBN 0-8225-0990-3 (lib. bdg.)
ISBN 0-8225-9546-X (pbk.)

Manufactured in the United States of America

    3   4   5   6   7   8   9   10   97   96   95   94   93   92   91   90

Susan: When is it polite to stick out your tongue?

Mary: At a doctor's office.

Patient: I'm as sick as a dog.
Doctor: I can't help you, I'm not a vet.

Mark: I think I have the chicken pox.
Sally: How can you tell?
Mark: There were feathers on my pillow
this morning.

Q: What do you call when you break your
foot?
A: A toe-truck.

Q: Why did the boy take his shoes to the doctor?

A: They had lost their tongues.

Q: Why are doctors so nice?
A: They never run out of patience (patients).

Q: What did the patient say to the doctor after her eye operation?
A: "It's good to see you."

Q: What color is an eye chart after an exam?
A: Red (read).

Q: Why did the potato go to the doctor?
A: It was having eye problems.

Q: Why did the doctor tiptoe past the medicine cabinet?

A: She didn't want to wake the sleeping pills.

Q: How are bees and iodine alike?

A: They both sting.

Doctor: Mix this medicine with apple juice so you won't taste it.

Patient: Good idea, I hate the taste of apple juice.

Q: What should you do when your eyes water?

A: Put on glasses.

Q: What do you call two fighting Valentine's Day cards?

A: A heart attack.

Q: Why was the vampire put in jail?

A: He tried to rob a blood bank.

Q: What did Dracula say to the dentist?

A: "Fangs to you, I feel better."

Q: When is a doctor the busiest?

A: After fall.

Q: What should you do if your knee is cold?
A: Wear a knee cap.

Patient: What should I take when I'm run down?

Doctor: The license number.

Q: What did the sign outside the dentist's office say?

A: "Filling station."

Q: Why did the dentist go back to school?

A: To brush up on teeth.

Q: Why did the window go to the doctor?
A: It had a pane.

Q: How is a prospector like a doctor?
A: They both know how to find veins.

Q: Why was the thermometer put in jail?
A: It took a boy's temperature.

Q: Why was the surgeon so funny?
A: She was a real cutup.

Q: What part of your body is the
silliest?
A: Your funny bone.

Q: Why did the man laugh during his operation?

A: The doctor had him in stitches.

Q: What is the difference between a high
mountain and a spoonful of medicine?
A: One is hard to get up and the other
is hard to get down.

Q: What did one tonsil say to the other?
A: "You better get dressed because the
doctor is taking us out tonight."

Q: What happened when the boy swallowed
a rope?
A: He became tongue-tied.

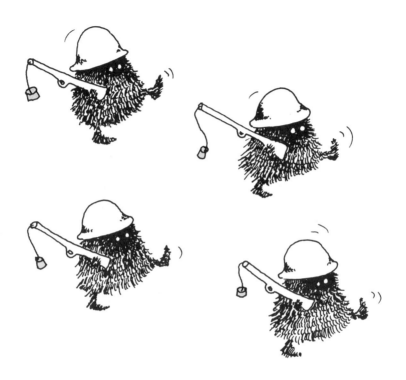

Q: What do you call it when you are fighting a cold?

A: Germ warfare.

Q: What is the best time to go to the dentist?
A: Tooth-hurty (2:30).

Q: How does a dentist fix a broken tooth?
A: Toothpaste.

Q: What did the dentist say in court?
A: I promise to tell the tooth, the whole tooth, and nothing but the tooth.

Q: Why did the king go to the dentist?
A: He needed a new crown.

Q: Why did the ship go to the doctor?
A: It was seasick.

Q: Why did the leopard go to the doctor?
A: He was covered with spots.

Mark: I'm seeing spots before my eyes.
Dave: Have you seen a doctor?
Mark: No, just spots.

Q: Why is a trap like the measles?
A: They're both catching.

Q: What did the doctor prescribe to get rid of the measles?

A: Spot remover.

Q: What color is a cold?
A: Blew.

Q: Why can't skeletons be doctors?
A: They have no stomach for it.

Q: What is the most popular name for a doctor?
A: Bill.

Q: Who do you see when you break a limb?
A: A tree surgeon.

Q: What do you call a cactus that isn't feeling well?

A: A sickly prickly.

Q: Why did the fisherman go to the doctor?
A: He wanted a good cast.

Q: Why did the short basketball player
  call the ambulance?
A: He wanted to use their stretcher.

Q: Why did the jogger go to the doctor?
A: For her 5,000-mile checkup.

Q: What did the runner say after she lost the race?

A: I have the agony of de-feet (defeat).

Knock, knock.
Who's there?
Acht.
Acht who?
Gesundheit.

Knock, knock.
Who's there?
Sarah.
Sarah who?
Sarah doctor in the house?

Knock, knock.
Who's there?
Vita.
Vita who?
Vit-a-min, we're having a party.

ABOUT THE AUTHORS

PETER AND CONNIE ROOP have enjoyed sharing jokes with students in the United States and Great Britain. When not joking around, Peter and Connie write books and articles. Traveling, camping, and reading with their children, Sterling and Heidi, are their favorite pastimes. Both graduates of Lawrence University, the Roops now live in Appleton, Wisconsin.

ABOUT THE ARTIST

JOAN HANSON lives with her husband and two sons in Afton, Minnesota. Her distinctive, deliberately whimsical pen-and-ink drawings have illustrated more than 30 children's books. Ms. Hanson is also an accomplished weaver. A graduate of Carleton College, Hanson enjoys tennis, skiing, sailing, reading, traveling, and walking in the woods surrounding her home.

Make Me Laugh!

CAN YOU MATCH THIS?
CAT'S OUT OF THE BAG!
CLOWNING AROUND!
DUMB CLUCKS!
ELEPHANTS NEVER FORGET!
FACE THE MUSIC!
FOSSIL FOLLIES!
GO HOG WILD!

GOING BUGGY!
GRIN AND BEAR IT!
HAIL TO THE CHIEF!
IN THE DOGHOUSE!
KISS A FROG!
LET'S CELEBRATE!
OUT TO LUNCH!
OUT TO PASTURE!
SNAKES ALIVE!
SOMETHING'S FISHY!
SPACE OUT!
STICK OUT YOUR TONGUE!
WHAT A HAM!
WHAT'S YOUR NAME?
WHAT'S YOUR NAME, AGAIN?
101 ANIMAL JOKES
101 FAMILY JOKES
101 KNOCK-KNOCK JOKES
101 MONSTER JOKES
101 SCHOOL JOKES
101 SPORTS JOKES